TO THE LIMIT

by Jeffrey Crelinsten

WIDE WORLD SERIES

Gulliver Books

Harcourt Brace Jovanovich, Publishers

San Diego   New York   London

This book is based on the OMNIMAX film To The Limit, *a production of the Museum Film Network and NOVA/WGBH Boston, produced by MacGillivray Freeman Films, from a film script by Jon Boorstin.*

Text and illustration compilation copyright © 1992 by Somerville House Books Ltd.
Text copyright © 1992 by Jeffrey Crelinsten
IMAX® photographs from the film *To The Limit* copyright © 1989 by Museum Film Network and WGBH
Educational Foundation

First U.S. edition 1992

Library of Congress Cataloging-in-Publication Data
Crelinsten, Jeffrey.
To the limit/by Jeffrey Crelinsten.
p. cm.
"Gulliver books."
Includes index.
Summary: Discusses how the systems in the human body work and how they are affected by exercise.
ISBN 0-15-200616-8
1. Exercise—Juvenile literature. 2. Physical fitness—Juvenile literature. [1. Physical fitness. 2. Body,
Human. 3. Exercise.]
I. Title.
QP301.C68   1992
612".044 — dc20 91-39796

IMAX® is a registered trademark of Imax Corporation, 38 Isabella Street, Toronto, Ontario, M4Y 1N1.

Produced by Somerville House Books Ltd., 3080 Yonge Street, Suite 5000, Toronto, Ontario, Canada M4N 3N1
Printed in Singapore
Design: Andrew Smith and Annabelle Stanley/Andrew Smith Graphics Inc., Toronto, Ontario
Illustrations by David Chapman
Indexing by Heather L. Ebbs

ABCDE

The author wishes to thank Paula Crelinsten for putting up with the late nights, and the following people for their
advice and comments: Dr. Anne Agur, Department of Anatomy, University of Toronto; David Moore, coordinator
of physical education, Etobicoke Board of Education, and avid climber; Jenny Glickman, who did a lot of the early
research on this book; Erica Glossop, for her insights about ballet; Betty Oliphant of The National Ballet School,
Toronto, for comments on chapter 4; and Colleen Zilio, Science North.

This book is an introduction to the human body for children. It is important that all learning experiences for children
be properly supervised by attending adults, be they parents, family members, teachers, or friends. This is especially
true when children are learning to use their bodies in new and unfamiliar ways, some of which may be mentally and
physically demanding and stressful. Please ensure that the children under your care are given the necessary level of
supervision and guidance appropriate for their age, size, and level of ability, judgment, and maturity.

Cover photograph: *Tony Yaniro uses a special climbing technique to scale a sheer rock face.*

Title page photograph: *Tony Yaniro hangs under a ledge in Yosemite Canyon.*

Opposite page: *Maria Walliser, as she makes her descent along the course at Aspen.*

CONTENTS

YOUR AMAZING BODY

A loud crack from home plate grabs your attention. Your mind jumps out of its outfielder's daydream and you stare down the field. Where is the ball? Suddenly you see it arching high into the air. It's coming straight for you. If you don't start running now, it'll sail right over your head.

Your body leaps into action. As you streak upfield, your legs and arms pump, your heart pounds, your breath goes in and out. Everything works together.

Most of the time we aren't aware that our bodies are doing anything special. Only when we push ourselves do we begin to notice. Running full tilt for that ball, you definitely notice your body working! You can feel your heart pumping and your lungs puffing. You may even feel perspiration on your skin — a sign that your body is trying to keep its temperature down.

The human body is an excellent instrument for doing things that require us to move — running, climbing, jumping, pulling, pushing, rolling, or tumbling. When an Olympic long jumper makes his jump, his body performs a symphony of movements, chemical reactions, and electrical activities that allow him to run and jump as fast and far as he can.

The same is true for your body as you race for that ball. You may not realize it, but thousands of different parts are actively working together so you can continue to run.

Your skeleton supports your body. It gives you your basic shape, protects your inner organs, and carries the skin and outer parts of your body. Your bones are connected at joints, which work like hinges to allow your bones to move in all sorts of different directions.

Your skeletal muscles are attached to your bones. When a muscle contracts, or tightens, it becomes shorter, and some part of you moves. Take your legs, for example. They pump up and down as you run for the ball. You bend your knees by contracting your hamstrings. You straighten them by contracting your quadriceps. This movement also stretches your hamstrings so they're ready to contract again. Every movement you make happens because your muscles contract and pull on your bones.

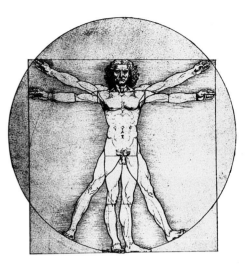

Above: *Painters and sculptors have been fascinated with the human body for centuries. This famous illustration, called* The Proportions of Man, *was drawn over 400 years ago by Leonardo da Vinci (1452–1519).*

Left: *Babe Ruth, probably one of the greatest hitters of all time, watches the ball after he's just slugged it. Note how his body is still turning from his powerful swing.*

Opposite page: *Planning his next move carefully, rock climber Tony Yaniro has to lean back to study the rock face towering above him.*

ANIMAL ATHLETES

In the animal world you can find some athletes that no human could ever beat. Ruby-throated hummingbirds fly 1,500 miles (2,400 kilometers) across the Gulf of Mexico in twenty-four hours. Their average speed over the entire day is 62 miles per hour (100 kilometers per hour) — as fast as a speeding train! Olympic marathon runners take more than two hours to run about 2 percent of that distance. Animals are faster sprinters, too. Olympic champion Carl Lewis holds the world sprinting record — 100 meters in about 9 seconds. That's an average speed of just over 10 meters per second, about 20 miles per hour. In 2 seconds a cheetah can accelerate to 45 miles per hour (72 kilometers per hour). That's 20 meters per second, or twice Carl's average sprinting speed. During a chase, a cheetah reaches peak speeds of about 70 miles per hour (112 kilometers per hour), or three times Carl's average speed.

And compare the best male Olympic pole vaulters, who can jump five times their height, to a flea, which can jump 200 times its body length in one jump!

While animals can usually outperform humans in one single activity, humans can excel in many different activities. We can sprint, run long distances, swim, jump, throw objects, and much more. The human body is well designed for a wide range of physical tasks. That's one reason we can adapt to so many different habitats and living conditions.

How did your muscles get the energy to make you run so well? When you sat down to eat your breakfast, it was as if you were putting gasoline in the tank of a car. No matter what meal you had — a gooey cheese omelet, a stack of pancakes dripping with syrup, or a bowl of cereal piled with fresh fruit — once it went down your throat, it was on its way to becoming fuel for your muscles and other parts of your body.

Chemicals in your stomach break down the food you eat. The carbohydrates are stored in muscle and liver cells. Fat is stored in fat cells. The muscles can convert both these fuels into energy. But to do this efficiently, they also need oxygen. Luckily, we live surrounded by a huge mixture of gases, called the atmosphere, which is 21 percent oxygen. You can feel the atmosphere on your face as you run. Every breath you take pulls air into your lungs. Oxygen from the air then passes from your lungs into blood cells.

Your heart, pounding away inside your chest, pumps these blood cells through tubes, called arteries, to every part of your body. As you run, your muscles need lots of oxygen, so your lungs and heart must work especially hard.

That batter sure hit the ball far! A pain starts to build in your side as you push yourself to the limit.

Your body is a wonderful, complex system that can do the most amazing things. But it's like a high-performance racing bike. Let your bike sit for weeks

Opposite page: *Even a friendly neighborhood basketball game can get your heart pounding and your lungs puffing.*

HOW FIT ARE YOU?

On a hike you can easily spot who's in good physical shape and who's not. The ones in good condition breathe more regularly. The ones who aren't huff and puff.

If you could go inside their bodies, you'd see more differences. The fit person's lungs and heart are working smoothly, efficiently, quietly. The unfit person's inner systems have to work much harder to collect oxygen and move it to their muscles.

Your heart pumps blood through your arteries. First it squeezes hard, squirting blood out. Blood surges into the arteries. The elastic walls of the arteries stretch to make room for the extra blood. Then the heart relaxes, and the blood flow from the heart slows for an instant. The arteries relax. Then the heart squeezes again, pushing more blood into the arteries.

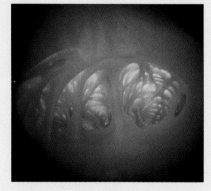

A view into the entry chamber of the heart, shot with a special telescopic steel tube.

The result is that blood flows throughout your body's network of arteries in a pulsing motion — surge, relax, surge, relax. The arteries expand, relax, expand, relax in the same rhythm. We call this rhythm our pulse.

Most of our arteries are buried deep inside the body. But in a few places, arteries run close to the skin. You can put a finger on these areas and feel your pulse.

The best spots are
— the inside of your wrist, below the thumb
— your neck, at the throat on either side of your Adam's apple

Put your fingers on one of these places to feel your pulse. Count the number of beats you get in ten seconds. Multiply the number by six to get the number of beats per minute. That number is your "resting" pulse. Most people's pulses are somewhere between sixty and eighty beats per minute. Athletes have much lower resting pulses. A trained swimmer's can be as low as forty, and long-distance runners can have even lower resting pulses.

Use your pulse to compare the amount of work it takes to do different activities, like sitting, lying down, standing on one leg, walking, running, climbing stairs, and so on. The more your muscles have to work, the faster your pulse will be. But if you're in good physical condition, your heart won't have to beat as fast to work hard. Compare your resting and active pulses with those of your friends. Who's in better shape?

or months without riding, greasing, or washing it, and you'll soon notice that it doesn't work as well as it used to. The same is true for your body.

Most of us don't push our bodies very much. We use them only as much as we need to. People usually prefer to take the bus or drive their car. They don't walk much. And they certainly don't run if they can help it. So their bodies don't work very hard.

People who exercise have better-developed bodies. Their lungs can take in air more quickly; their hearts beat more strongly and might even be bigger; their blood flows more easily; their muscles are stronger and work more efficiently. That's why you usually feel healthier when you exercise regularly. In recent years, marathon running has become very popular. Hundreds of people show up for the major events. They use long-distance running as a way to keep their bodies in good working condition.

Our bodies actually change the more we use them. Look at professional athletes. These people push their bodies to the limit. A runner wants to run faster than anyone else. A pole vaulter wants to vault the highest. A baseball player wants to hit a home run or catch a fly ball. Whatever sport an athlete does, his or her body changes in a particular way. A wrestler will have large arm and chest muscles. A runner will have well-developed leg muscles and a strong heart. Athletes are generally in terrific shape.

Training for a professional sport is tough. You have to work on your entire body — your lungs, your heart, your muscles, even your mind. Some people say that

Opposite page: *Microscopic view of tiny capillaries in human tissue. The large bubbles are fat cells.*

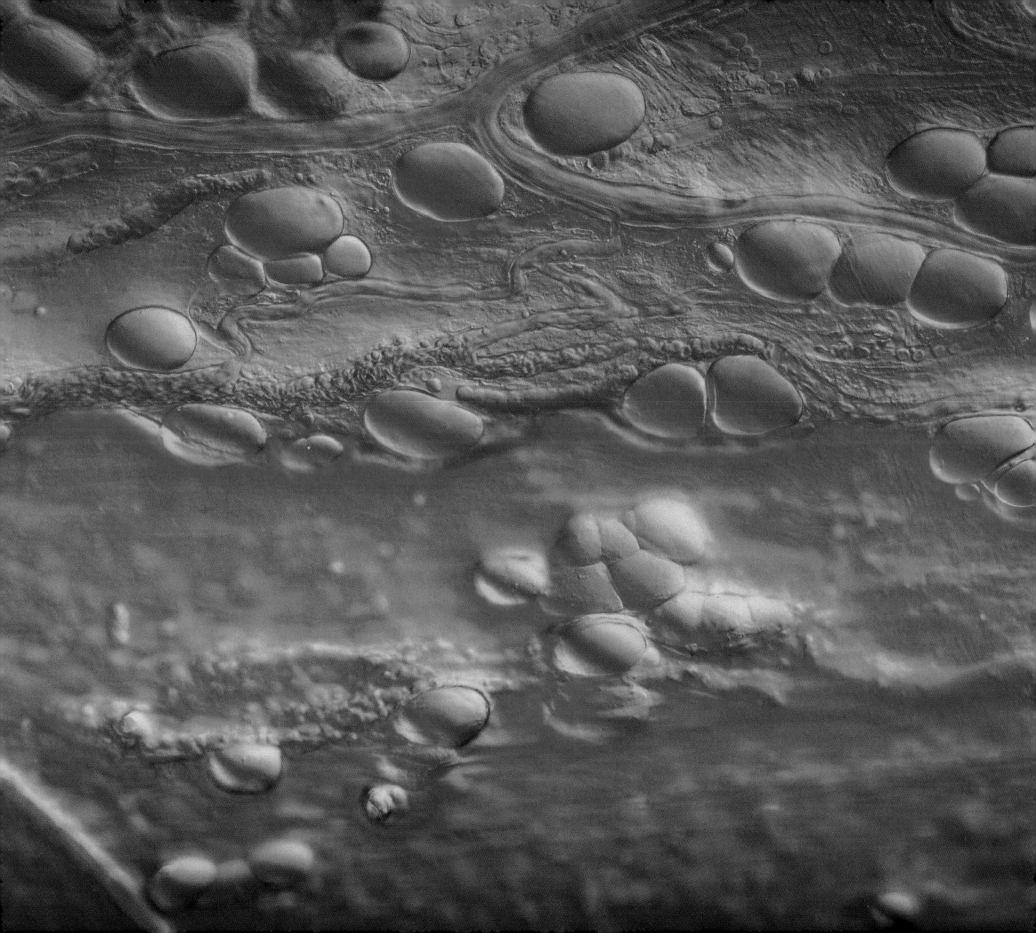

one of the most important and difficult aspects of sports is the mental part. Athletes have to be able to concentrate. They have to be aware of their bodies and how they are moving. Athletes must be alert at every instant.

LOOKING INSIDE THE BODY

A bunch of optical fibers, each strand as thin as a human hair. Light travels down each strand. These optical fibers can be used to look inside the human body.

You can't look inside your body to see what's wrong — but your doctor can!

In 1957 two American medical scientists built the world's first modern *fiberscope*. They used it to look inside a person's body at the stomach and esophagus (the tube leading from the throat to the stomach). Since then, more ingenious devices have been built that can examine any organ system in the body.

The fiberscope was made possible by the invention of optical fibers — so thin and flexible that they look like strands of a spider's web. Actually they're very pure glass, made from silica. If you shine light into one end, a beam will travel down the length of the fiber and come out the other end.

The glass in your bedroom window lets in light, but it also absorbs a lot of it. If you made it as thick as an elephant, most light wouldn't get through. An optical fiber lets 10,000 times more light through than normal glass. If you shone a bright light at one end of an optical fiber several city blocks in length, you'd still see light coming out the other end.

A fiberscope is made of two bundles of optical fibers. Each bundle contains thousands of fibers, yet the bundle is still less than a millimeter in diameter. The doctor shines light down one bundle. The light is reflected from whatever is at the other end and comes back up the second fiber bundle. Each fiber carries a tiny piece of the image, and together they bring back a complete picture. The doctor looks through a lens and sees a perfect image of the inside of the body.

Fighting your pain, your mind forces you to keep going. The roar of the crowd gets louder. The ball is near. You slow down. There it is! Out goes your glove and — thump — you've made the catch.

Only after you've thrown the ball back do you realize that your heart is still pounding. Your chest is heaving and your breath is coming fast. Your body is still in high gear, and it will take a few minutes to get back to the state it was in before you started to run for the ball.

Your body is a fantastic machine. It will do the most amazing things for you. But you have to learn how to use your body properly. If you do, it may even perform miracles for you — like running and catching that ball!

Above: *What a catch! Ty Cobb was one of the greatest American baseball players of all time. His amazing career spanned 24 years from 1905 to 1928. Here we see him leaping into the air to make the grab.*

Opposite page: *Thousands of people turned up for this marathon race in New York City.*

YOUR INNER BODY

People look different from one another. If you compare their faces, how they dress, the way they walk — they're all individuals. But inside, our bodies all work in the same way.

The human body is incredibly complex. Every separate part of the body has a special use. But all the parts work together as a whole, because they make up a larger system. It's like a team. Every part works together with every other part.

The skeleton is the main support for the team. It is both strong and flexible. Our skull is tough and hard, so it can protect the brain inside. Our rib cage guards our inner organs. Our spine protects the spinal cord, which runs from our brain to our lower body. While the bones themselves are strong and inflexible, many joints between them allow us to move around easily.

Muscles of all shapes and sizes are attached to the bones.

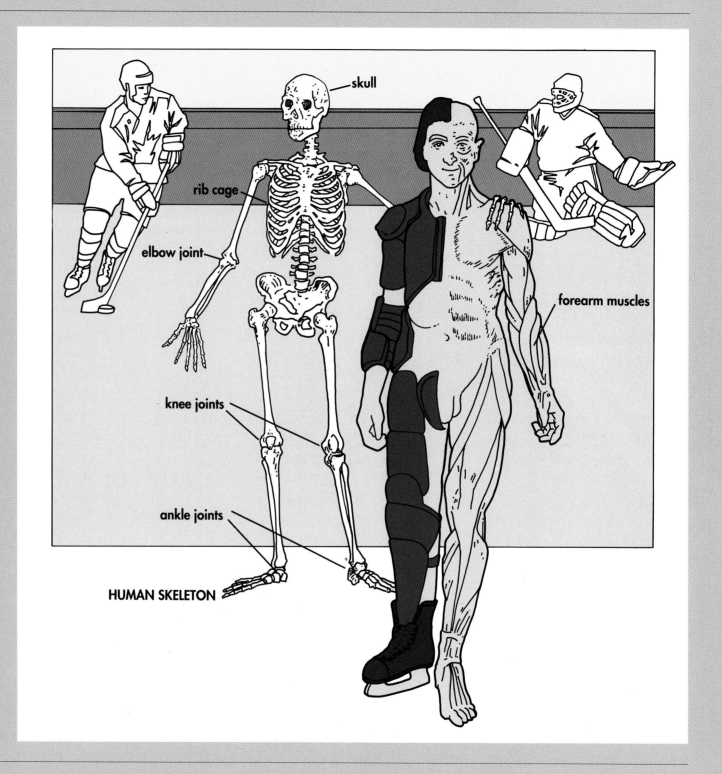

HUMAN SKELETON

These muscles, called *skeletal muscles,* make up nearly half your body weight. They're also called *voluntary muscles,* because you can decide when to use them. Skeletal muscles are what we use to move.

Other muscles work automatically, without any decisions from you. They're called *involuntary muscles.* Your heart will pump nonstop throughout your lifetime. It will contract and relax about two and a half billion times by the time you reach eighty years old.

Your heart is the star of the circulatory system — a complex network of arteries and veins that carries blood from the heart to all parts of the body and back again. The heart receives blood cells that have just picked up oxygen from the lungs. It pumps these oxygen-carrying blood cells through arteries all around the body. Once the oxygen is used up by muscles and other tissues, veins carry the blood cells back to the heart and then to the lungs, where they receive more oxygen.

The lungs are also stars of the respiratory system, which is responsible for collecting oxygen from the air and getting it into the blood cells. Air enters your nose and mouth and travels down your windpipe into your lungs. Oxygen passes from your lungs into your blood cells.

The respiratory, circulatory, muscular, and skeletal systems all work together to allow you to move around in the world. Other systems make up the rest of the team, bringing information from the outside world to your brain so you know how to plan your moves.

Your visual system brings images of the world through your eyes. Your ears bring sounds to your brain. Your skin covers your entire body in a protective blanket. It can sense the outside world by contact or by feeling heat radiated from objects — including the distant sun. Your nose collects samples of gas from the outside world and tells your brain a lot about the environment and nearby objects. And your tongue can also sense chemicals that come in contact with it.

The captain of the entire team of body systems and parts

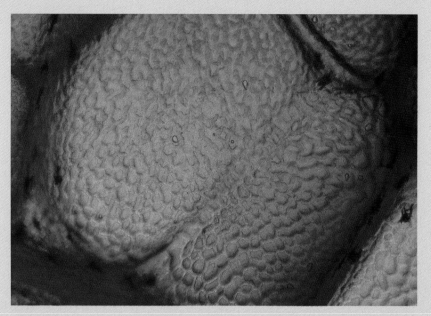

Closeup of tiny air sacs (called alveoli) *inside the lung, surrounded by tiny blood vessels (called* capillaries). *Oxygen seeps through the walls of the alveoli and the capillaries into the bloodstream.*

is your brain. Your brain directs and controls everything that goes on in your body. It communicates through a system of nerves called the nervous system. The spinal cord is like the main telephone line that allows signals to move between the brain and other parts of the body. But there are millions of other nerve cells in your body. These long, spindly cells connect to one another, forming a complex web of communication pathways. They carry electrical signals to and from the brain. Some connect to the spinal cord, and others form their own smaller highways.

Your body is much more complicated than a hockey or baseball team, or even a team of aerospace engineers building a spacecraft. It is made up of trillions of cells — as many as there are stars in five hundred galaxies. All these cells work together to help you to do even the simplest act — like sitting comfortably and reading this book.

SCALING THE HEIGHTS

Tony Yaniro looks like a tiny bug against the huge expanse of sheer rock. The muscles in his fingers and hands and a narrow ledge under his toes are all that keep him from falling. His arms stretch out as if to give the cliff an enormous hug. Strong fingers probe for cracks or tiny knobs of rock to grab for balance. To his right a torrent of water thunders past on its way to the depths below. Tony inches to his left, looking for a safe spot to continue his climb.

Rock climbing is like a vertical dance. Your body must be in good shape and your mind clear and alert. "What I'm trying to do is solve a puzzle," Tony explains. "Not just mentally, but physically."

The puzzle is how to work his way up the mountain before his muscles run out of energy. Tony knows that if he pushes too long without a rest, his muscles will quit. "I know I only have so much time. I have to know my limits."

Tony's muscles need a good supply of oxygen. Every minute his powerful lungs must draw in about a gallon (four liters) of oxygen from the thin mountain air. His lungs transfer the oxygen to his blood cells. His heart pumps the blood to his muscles.

If the supply of oxygen becomes too low or if he pushes himself too far, Tony's muscles will stop working. A climber's worst nightmare is to watch helplessly as his fingers slowly let go of a handhold. He knows he will fall, but he can't do anything about it. His muscles have simply given out. That's why experienced climbers always use ropes for safety.

Even though most climbers develop strong arm and hand muscles, experienced climbers try to let their legs do most of the work. They use their upper body as sparingly as they can. That way, their arm and hand muscles will last longer. Moves are planned ahead in a sequence. When the climbers are ready, they move through each one as quickly as they can, flowing from one to the other. Stopping and starting burns up energy, just as driving a car in rush-hour traffic uses up lots of gasoline.

Tony continues along the ledge, moving sideways, pressed against the rock. The sun is going to set soon. If he can't make it to the top before then, he'll have to sleep on the cliff. He looks up and sees a long vertical crack slicing right through the rock above him. He decides to use it as a "chimney."

Left: In 1953, British climber Sir Edmund Hillary's expedition was the first to reach the summit of Mt. Everest, the highest mountain in the world.

Opposite page: Tony Yaniro uses a special climbing technique to scale a sheer rock face.

MUSCLE POWER

Without muscles, we couldn't breathe, digest food, walk, or even blink. Every movement we make is caused by a muscle getting shorter. Muscle is the only tissue in our bodies that can do this. All the other kinds of tissue — skin, hair, bone, cartilage — stay the same size unless they are growing. When a muscle gets shorter we say it contracts, and some part of us moves.

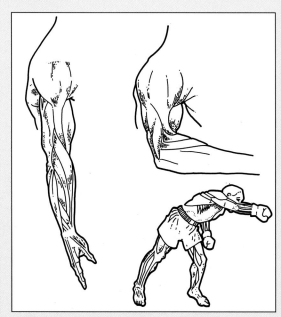

Skeletal muscles become larger and more powerful with use. A boxer develops strong arm, chest, and leg muscles.

When you stand on a scale, nearly half your weight comes from your *skeletal muscles*. These muscles, also called *striated muscles*, are attached to your bones. You use them for breathing and to move your limbs, head, and other parts of your body. If you want to wiggle your toes, your brain sends signals to the muscles in your feet. These signals tell the muscles to contract. As the muscles get shorter, they pull on the bones in your toes and the toes move.

Hold this book in your left hand straight out in front of you. Raise it up by bending your elbow and let it down again. Now put your right hand lightly on your upper arm and lift and lower the book again. To lift the book, you contract a muscle called a biceps in your upper arm. You can feel the muscle becoming thicker as it shortens. As your biceps contracts, your triceps — a muscle on the opposite side of your arm — stretches.

When you lower the book, your triceps contracts, and you can feel your biceps relax again.

We have two other kinds of muscle in our bodies. *Smooth muscles* move our internal organs. Some smooth muscles help move blood through our veins and arteries. Others move food through our intestines. Smooth muscles are often involuntary muscles — they work without any conscious control from us.

The heart is a third kind of muscle, called *cardiac muscle* — and a most amazing muscle it is. It pumps blood to every nook and cranny of your body and back again. As long as you live, your heart never stops working.

Tony wedges himself inside the vertical crack, or "chimney," by pushing his back against one side and his feet against the other. He moves up by pushing down on one foot, just as if he's walking, and sliding his back up the opposite wall.

Pushing constantly in opposite directions puts a lot of strain on Tony's leg and back muscles. On his way up, he takes long, deep breaths to keep the oxygen flowing to his muscles. He has to rest several times. During rests, Tony's heart slows down. His breathing returns to normal, and his muscles relax.

Finally Tony is at the top of the crack. He stretches his aching limbs and looks up. The last stretch to the top will be difficult. Tony decides this will have to be his last effort for the day.

After sunset the temperature plummets. Tony is wearing several layers of loose clothing to trap air around his body for insulation. He eats a good meal, suspends his sleeping bag from a support he hammers into the rock face, climbs in, and goes to sleep.

As Tony sleeps, his body continues to work. Vessels carrying blood to the outer parts of his body narrow. More blood can then flow to his internal organs, which continue to need oxygen. His digestive system breaks down the food he ate and stores some for later use. And his muscles rest.

When morning comes, Tony is refreshed. Now it is time to tackle the toughest part of the climb. The route to the top is blocked by a ledge of rock, called an overhang, that sticks straight out of the cliff.

Overhangs are the hardest on a climber's arms

Opposite page: *The sun glistens behind Tony's darkened silhouette as he "chimneys" up a long vertical crack in the rock.*

and upper body. His feet are no longer underneath him, so his leg muscles can't carry his weight. Tony anchors the end of his safety rope in the rock. He draws a deep breath, grabs the ledge, and starts to move. Almost immediately, one foot loses its hold and his leg dangles uselessly. Experience tells him to keep moving. Inching slowly with his hands, he lets his weight hang on the bones and tendons in his upper body. An inexperienced climber would pull up and quickly exhaust his energy.

Just as Tony is about to reach his target, his hands slip on some loose pebbles. Instantly, he realizes he's going to fall. As he plummets, he relaxes and prepares for the jerk as the rope breaks his fall. A surge of adrenaline sharpens his senses. Will the rope hold?

Oomph! The breath is forced out of him as the rope yanks his body to a stop. Dangling on the end, Tony looks up and sees that the rope is caught far above him by a sharp edge of rock. Below him, rocks seem to spin eerily as he sways and turns like a fish on a line. The cliff seems to circle around and around him — always beyond his reach.

Quickly, Tony starts to swing his body back and forth. As he nears the rock face, he tries to grab it with one foot, but he can't get a grip. He swings away. Again he grabs, and again he misses. He looks up. The rope is being worn away by the sharp rock. This time he has to make it. As he swings against the rock face, Tony jams the side of his foot down against a small ledge. It holds. He bends his legs to pull his body toward the rock. First one hand grabs. Then the other. He's safe. Just then, high above, the rope snaps and tumbles past him.

An amazing calm comes over Tony as the adrenaline leaves his blood system. He looks up, inhales deeply, and feels very much alive!

Opposite page: *Tony works his way along a ledge. He hammers supports into the rock to hold his safety rope.*

THE AMAZING CHEMICAL — ATP

The flight muscles in a housefly, the mold growing on an old sandwich, and a rock climber's arm muscles all get their energy from the same chemical. It's called *adenosine triphosphate,* or ATP.

A small amount of ATP exists in all our muscles. When ATP in a muscle combines with water, it breaks down into two parts — ADP (adenosine diphosphate) and phosphate. A tiny amount of energy is released, and the muscle uses that energy to contract. Every time a runner takes a step, a hundred million trillion ATP molecules change to ADP and phosphate.

The harder our muscles work, the more ATP they need. More ATP can be made by combining ADP and phosphate — the very same chemicals that were produced when ATP released energy for the muscles. The energy to make more ATP comes from the food we eat.

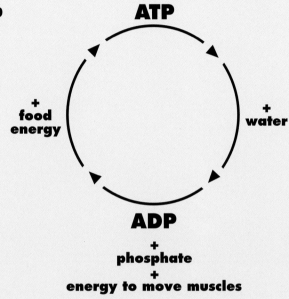

The ATP cycle. Energy from the food you eat is used to combine the chemical ADP with phosphate to produce ATP. Your muscles break down the ATP in order to move. The waste products from this reaction are ADP and phosphate — the very chemicals needed to make more ATP.

If we demand too much from our muscles, ATP can't be made fast enough. Our muscles start to ache, and we get tired. We slow down, even if we don't want to. Our bodies are sending a message: Stop now before all the energy is used up. If you still keep pushing, the odds are you might simply pass out. Our bodies stop us from going beyond our limits.

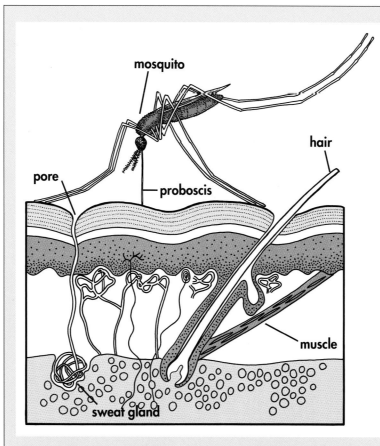

SKIN: THE BODY'S THERMOSTAT

Your skin is not simply a handy bag to carry your bones and insides around. It's a vital organ of your body — the largest one you've got. And it changes all the time, so you can feel cool as a cucumber or warm as toast, depending on what you need.

If your body gets too hot, blood vessels in your skin open wider to let more blood flow through them. Larger amounts of blood get into the tiny channels, called capillaries, near the surface so more heat can escape into the air. This is why your skin turns red when you are hot.

Your skin also sweats when you're too warm. Sweat glands buried in the deep layers of your skin receive fluid from the surrounding capillaries. They pass the fluid through a spiral passageway that opens onto the skin's surface as a sweat pore. When the sweat evaporates into the air, it cools your skin.

What happens if you're cold? Again your skin adapts. The walls of some blood vessels contract so less blood can flow to the capillaries near the surface and less heat can escape. This is why we turn pale when we're

On the left, a pore leads down to a sweat gland buried in the deep layer of the skin. On the right a long muscle is attached to the base of a hair that tilts to the right. When it contracts, it pulls the base of the hair to the right, causing the hair to stand up straight. A mosquito perches on the skin surface.

cold and sometimes even turn blue. Sweating stops so that less heat is lost by evaporation. And tiny muscles attached to the base of the hairs contract, pulling on the hairs and making them stand on end. This causes the skin to be covered in "goose bumps." In hairy animals, the standing hair traps more air, which insulates the body.

The larger the surface of skin open to the air, the more heat escapes from your body. Animals trying to keep warm curl their bodies in a tight ball. This reduces the area of their bodies exposed to air. You do the same thing when you curl up on a cold winter's night in front of the fire.

Opposite page: *The sheer rock face plunges straight down beneath Tony's feet as he inches himself up along a crack.*

ADRENALINE RUSH

Climbers develop strong hands and forearms from holding onto tiny cracks. Notice the perspiration on Tony's forearm.

Just as you grasp a handhold, your foot slips under you. Before you know it, you're hanging on the cliff face, holding on with one hand. A sinking feeling hits the pit of your stomach. You're in a cold sweat, and your hair is standing on end. You're terrified that you're going to fall. But with a strength you never thought you had, you pull yourself up with one arm, while your feet scramble for a foothold. Safe once more, you realize your heart is still pounding and you are breathing fast. You've just had an adrenaline rush.

In an emergency, special glands sitting above your kidneys send out a hormone called *adrenaline*. This chemical quickly makes your heart beat faster to get blood to the muscles. Many small blood vessels contract, like ones in your skin (so your skin turns pale) and in your gut (so you get that sinking feeling). More blood starts to flow to your muscles and your lungs, where it is needed most. Your mouth opens to take in more air, and your breathing rate speeds up to get more oxygen into your bloodstream. And you start to sweat to keep cool.

Climbers get this reaction whenever they are in a dangerous situation. The adrenaline rush lets them do things they could never do otherwise. They can move faster, pull themselves higher, grab more quickly, reach farther, and hold on longer.

When the danger is over, the adrenaline disappears quickly. Climbers feel relaxed and happy, even euphoric, as if they've just done something amazing — and they usually have!

Above: *Adrenaline courses through Tony's body as he falls. Tony relaxes as best he can, hoping his safety rope will hold when it breaks his fall.*

Opposite page: *The rope holds. Now Tony must try to swing back to safety on the rock face.*

THE LUNGS — OUR OXYGEN COLLECTORS

All the cells in our bodies need oxygen. They also have to get rid of carbon dioxide, which is a waste product from their activities. Our veins and arteries make up the main highway system, which is called the *circulatory system*. Blood travels on this highway, carrying oxygen to and carbon dioxide from the cells.

But how does our body get oxygen into the blood system and carbon dioxide back out? Our *respiratory system* does this job.

Right: The windpipe carries air in and out of your lungs through a complicated network of tubes. These tubes divide into smaller and smaller branches that eventually lead to tiny sacs called alveoli.

Upper left: A network of tiny capillaries surround each alveolus. Oxygen passes through the walls of the alveoli and through the capillary walls into the bloodstream.

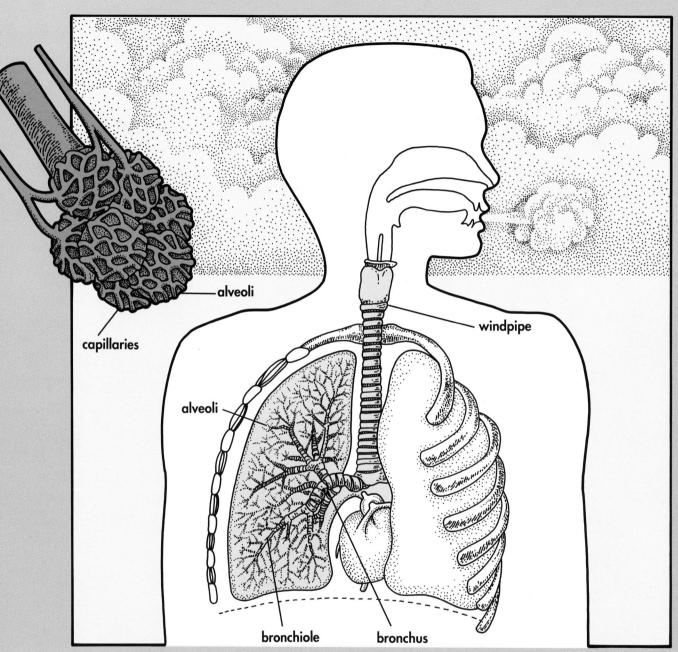

capillaries

alveoli

alveoli

windpipe

bronchiole

bronchus

Air enters your body through your nose and mouth. Your nose filters, warms, and moistens the air. It also examines the air chemically for any substance that might irritate the lining of the tunnel leading to the lungs. Your throat is the "hallway" to this tunnel, which is lined with little hairs and mucus that help to filter the air even more as it continues to the lungs.

The throat opens into a box-like area called the *larynx*. The larynx is your body's traffic cop, directing air to the lungs and food to the stomach. Whenever food comes in, a small flap of cartilage called the *epiglottis* snaps shut. This prevents particles or liquids from going into your lungs. Instead they pass safely down another tube into your stomach. Another important role your larynx plays is to produce your voice. That's why it's also called the voice box.

The larynx leads to the *trachea*, or windpipe, which channels air into your lungs. The trachea divides at its lower end into two branches, called the *primary bronchi*. Each one enters a lung and immediately

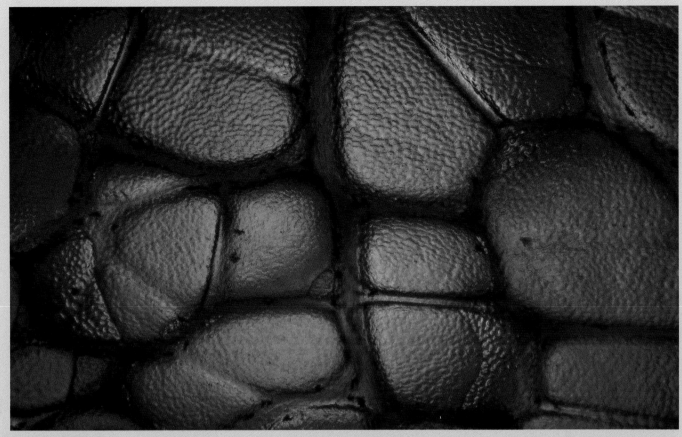

This photograph of the surface of the lung shows blood vessels carrying oxygen-bearing blood from the lungs to the rest of the body.

divides into several smaller branches, called *secondary bronchi*. These continue to branch, eventually forming small *bronchioles*. If you look at a picture of the trachea, the bronchi, and the bronchioles, you will see that they look like an upside-down tree.

The bronchioles continue to divide into smaller and smaller tubes until they are so tiny that you can see them only under a microscope. The ends of these minute branches are called *alveoli*; they look like bunches of grapes. The walls of the alveoli are very thin. They are surrounded by a network of capillaries. Oxygen passes through the walls of the alveoli and through the capillary walls into the bloodstream.

We have about half a billion alveoli in our two lungs. If you could spread out the walls of all the alveoli and put them together in one large sheet, they would cover the floor of a medium-sized room. That's why our lungs can transfer so much oxygen into our bloodstream and get the carbon dioxide out so quickly.

SPRINTING MUSCLE AND MARATHON MUSCLE

Why is a sprinter like a partridge and a marathon runner like a duck? The answer lies in their muscles.

We have two different kinds of skeletal muscles. One kind needs oxygen to turn food into energy. The other kind can get energy from stored food without the use of oxygen.

If you have to escape quickly from a dangerous situation, you have to use the second kind of muscle. Food fuel stored in your muscles is used immediately to produce energy. There's no time for your lungs and heart to get oxygen to your leg muscles.

Athletes use these muscles to make a quick sprint when they are playing baseball or basketball. The same is true for an Olympic sprinter like Carl Lewis, who runs fast and hard for a short time. Sprinters develop huge leg muscles, made mostly of the type that doesn't need oxygen.

But there's a limit to how long these muscles can work without oxygen. When very little oxygen is available to working muscles, a chemical called lactic acid is produced. If a lot of lactic acid builds up, it will prevent the muscle from contracting. That's what happens in your arms when you do lots of chin-ups, or in your legs when you run really fast. If not enough oxygen is present, lactic acid builds up quickly. Soon you feel pain and fatigue. That's the reason sprinters cannot run full tilt for very long and why climbers have to rest their arms and hands.

In certain activities, like cycling, swimming, and long-distance running, there's plenty of time to bring enough oxygen to the muscles. The oxygen is used by muscles to break down fuel. Muscles can also use the oxygen to break down lactic acid. That's the reason a marathon runner can go for so long without getting tired.

Animals also have both these kinds of muscle. When you peel off the skin of a grilled trout, you'll notice a thin line

of red muscle against the bulk of white muscle. The red muscle — marathon muscle, which needs oxygen — is used by the fish for long-distance swimming and normal cruising. The white muscle — sprinting muscle, which doesn't need oxygen — is used for abrupt, short escape movements, like fighting to get free from a fishhook.

A good angler will not fight against a fish that's wrestling to get off the hook. The angler knows that the fish is using its powerful sprinting muscles for the battle and lets the fish thrash around. Eventually lactic acid builds up in the muscle and the fish gets tired.

All animals, including humans, have both kinds of muscle. But athletes develop differently, depending on what they use their muscles for. A long-distance marathon runner develops more red muscle, which is specialized for using oxygen to produce energy. Sprinters develop more white muscle, which is especially good at producing energy without oxygen.

Partridge have mostly white sprinting muscle in their breasts. These muscles are used for the explosive bursts of energy needed to fly quickly to safety. Ducks, on the other hand, can fly hundreds of miles without stopping. These birds are flying marathoners. Their breast muscles are mostly of the red type.

Opposite page: Sprinter Gary Reid shoots out of the blocks, getting a good start in the 400 meter heat. Quick reflexes and muscle power are what make sprinters win races.

Right: Marathon runner Gary Westgate crosses the finish line to win the race. Pacing and endurance are what make long-distance runners win races.

27

RACING DOWN THE SLOPES

Maria Walliser no longer hears the noise of the portable radios, the helicopters, or the cheering crowds. As she waits in the darkness for the signal to start her run, she hears only the pounding of her own heart. In a few moments she will be hurtling down the steep slope to the quaint village of Aspen. In her mind she's already racing down the hill. Her body feels the perfect turns, the stretching of her muscles, the banging and clattering of her skis on the packed snow and ice, the blurring of vision from the vibrations.

"Thirty seconds!" The voice of the starter brings Maria back from her mental run. Maria's masseur is rubbing her right leg, warming the muscles for their coming torture. "Beatrice is down," he tells her. "Those steep, icy turns." Maria nods, disappointed to hear that her teammate Beatrice Gaffner has fallen.

"Ten seconds!" Her heart is racing now. Adrenaline is coursing through her blood. She slides forward

into the gate. "It will be perfect," she repeats softly to herself as her mind gets ready for the sudden rush of cold mountain air that will howl in her ears. *Beep, beep*, goes the electronic timer. And she's off!

World-class skiers like Maria Walliser have to master a new course each week. At Aspen she had only a few trial runs to figure out all the turns.

Downhill ski racing, like rock climbing, presents a puzzle. Champion skiers will tell you that races are won during the early inspection of the course and the trial runs. During the inspection, Maria and her coach inched their way down the course. They stopped often and tried to remember all the details of the run. How did the shape of the hill change? What was the fastest line through the turns? How did the snow feel?

After the inspection, all the skiers stand around the finish line, planning their moves. Their task is to memorize the entire course and figure out how their bodies and muscles will have to move.

Left: In the early 1900s women's skiing fashions were quite different from the nylon and Velcro of today.

Opposite page: Swiss champion skier Maria Walliser streaks down the alpine slope, leaving a trail of blowing snow in her wake.

PASTA AND FAT GO A LONG WAY!

If your body could use all the fat that it carries, you could run for about sixty-seven hours. But after running for more than ten minutes, most people are exhausted. Why?

Like oxygen, food fuels are carried to your muscles by blood flowing through the circulatory system. There are two main types of fuel — fatty acids and sugar.

Fatty acids are stored in fat cells. When energy is needed, the fatty acids enter the bloodstream and travel to the muscles. But blood can carry only a very small amount of fatty acids at one time. They can never get to our muscles quickly enough to let us run at top speed.

Sugar, in the form of glucose, is the fastest source of energy for muscles. That's why eating a chocolate bar can give you a quick boost. But your body doesn't store glucose. Where can you get extra fuel for a long race?

Complex carbohydrates — the same chemicals that make up pasta, potatoes, breads, and cereals — are easily stored in our bodies in the form of *glycogen*. Glycogen is made up of thousands of glucose units. Some glycogen is stored directly in our muscles — enough to let us run for about one hour and ten minutes. Extra glycogen kept in our liver can add another twenty minutes.

But a marathon lasts for more than two hours. When the glycogen runs out, runners typically feel as if they've run into an invisible wall. No matter how hard they push, they can't keep up the pace. Against their will, they have to slow down. That's because the only fuel that's left is fatty acids, which get to muscles very slowly.

Champion marathon runners don't "hit the wall." Their training has changed their bodies so that they can use more fatty acids during the race. Their glycogen is also used up more slowly and rarely runs out.

Now you know why marathon runners love pasta parties!

Marathon runners burn up food more efficiently than most other athletes. Their bodies learn to use more fat as fuel, so that other fuels such as glucose and glycogen are used up more slowly.

During Maria's first training run, she put her theories to the test. Not all of them passed. She had to make some changes. Especially during the corkscrew turns at the beginning. Some of the time she was flying in the air, and all her previous decisions about how she would turn and lean on her skis were useless.

During the days before the race, Maria went over and over the course in her mind. "I think about how I enter each turn, about each jump, each ice patch." After her final practice run, Maria had it worked out right.

Then she programmed her brain by imagining a perfect run over and over again. If she wasn't satisfied, she backed up her mental videotape and did a rerun — only perfectly this time. Every race she skied in her mind had to be perfect.

Now hurtling down the mountain, Maria has no time for doubts. Her body and mind have to work together. As she races into the corkscrew turns, the sports announcers go wild. "Boy, look at Walliser get back on her skis," someone shouts into his microphone. "Oh, she was great . . . turned right in the air . . . this is quite a ride!"

As the fans cheer, they have no idea of the punishment Maria's body is experiencing. Her powerful legs vibrate like jackhammers. Her skis rattle and her head vibrates up and down, blurring her vision. The gates that mark her turns are barely visible to her as she whizzes past. The wind howls in her helmet, and her ears ring.

Opposite page: Maria Walliser's view from the starting hut. When she hears the signal, she will jump forward into the abyss.

DANGEROUS SHORTCUTS

Some Olympic athletes and their trainers have figured out a dangerous way to increase the amount of oxygen reaching marathon runners' muscles. It is illegal in competition and physically hazardous, but people still do it.

A couple of months before the race, enough blood is removed from the athlete's body to fill a container the size of a large pop bottle. The blood is then specially treated and frozen. Since the athlete's body now has fewer red blood cells than normal, the brain sends a signal to increase production of red blood cells. After about five weeks the amount returns to normal. Then the frozen blood is thawed out and put back into the blood system. The athlete now has lots of extra red blood cells.

Red blood cells contain an important chemical called hemoglobin. Hemoglobin carries large amounts of oxygen through the bloodstream to the muscles. Some athletes find that with more hemoglobin, their endurance goes up. And that's sometimes enough to make the difference between winning and losing a race.

This technique, called blood doping, has been used by athletes such as runners and cyclists who need to keep going for long periods. At the 1984 Olympic Games, several members of the U.S. cycling team admitted to doping their blood. Since then the technique has been banned by the International Olympic Committee.

Unfortunately, some athletes also use drugs to change their bodies to perform better. Anabolic steroids for building muscle strength in sprinters and weight lifters are the best known of these illegal drugs. Using drugs to improve performance is a form of cheating and goes against the spirit of the Olympic Games. Even worse, these drugs often have harmful side effects and can damage athletes' bodies permanently. The International Olympic Committee has a network of medical laboratories around the world testing various drugs and finding ways to detect them in athletes' bodies.

Upper right: *The world tilts crazily as Maria digs the edges of her skis into the snow to make the turn.*

Opposite page: *The world whizzes by in a blur as Maria Walliser hurtles down the slope.*

Subtle changes in sound and vision tell Maria how to move. She digs the razor-sharp edge of her skis into the icy snow to make her turns. Too much and she'll slow down and lose precious time. Too little and she'll fall. Her leg muscles burn with pain as enormous forces pull on them during the sharp, fast turns.

Maria's heart pumps blood through arteries into her legs, bringing needed oxygen to her muscles.

Years of training have strengthened her heart and expanded the vast network of capillaries that feed every part of her legs, ankles, feet, and even her toes.

"Look at her accelerate! If she can hold it now on these steep, icy turns, she can move into the lead."

Maria knows she has to keep up her pace. She rockets into the turns, moving as fast as a car speeding down a major highway. *Dig with the skis! Lean hard! Turn! Right. Left.*

CAPILLARIES — THE BACKROADS OF THE CIRCULATORY SYSTEM

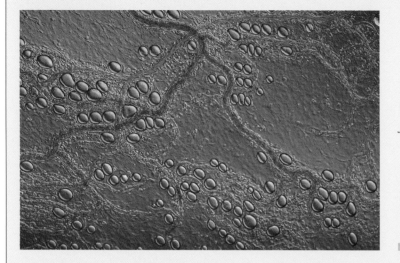

Tiny blood vessels called capillaries carry oxygen from the lungs to every living part of our body. They also carry carbon dioxide back to our lungs to be sent back outside.

If you lined up all the arteries, veins, and capillaries that make up your circulatory system, you could circle the earth's equator more than two times!

The reason all these different kinds of blood-carrying tubes fit inside your body is because of the way they are connected. Have you ever pulled a plant out of the ground? Roots divide into smaller and smaller roots, which all end with tiny hairs. Your circulatory system has a similar structure. The capillaries are like the tiny root hairs. The difference is that your capillaries are connected in an unending loop, whereas plant roots have ends.

Capillaries are so small you can't see them well without a microscope. Some of the tiniest ones are only the thickness of one blood cell. The capillaries deliver fuel and oxygen to all cells in the body. They also carry away the wastes. You can find capillaries surrounding any place in your body that needs energy, including your muscles.

Trained athletes develop large muscles. Which ones grow depends on the particular sport. Weight lifters have huge arm and chest muscles. Skiers have big leg muscles. Since these muscles need extra large amounts of energy, the body grows more capillaries near them to deliver lots of oxygen and fuel quickly. Runners and skiers develop thousands of tiny blood vessels in their legs, where they're needed most. Climbers will develop them in their hands and arms as well as in their lower bodies.

If athletes stop training because they've had an injury or have decided to retire, the extra capillaries will simply disappear. Because the muscles no longer demand so much energy, the body quickly closes up those delivery lines that aren't needed anymore.

Nearing the finish line, Maria has only a few turns left. She leans and digs the edges of her skis in for the turn, but not too much because she doesn't want to slow down. *Turn, turn!* her mind shrieks at her skis. The red fence marking the boundaries of the track looms in front of her. She pushes her edges harder into the ice and snow. *Turn!* The fence is still there, only larger. *Dig. Turn!*

Suddenly blue sky fills Maria's vision, as her legs slide out from under her. In slow motion, the world turns over and over — blue, then white, blue, white. Maria's mind is racing. Her entire body can feel the turn that went wrong. Not enough tension on the muscles and tendons. Not enough pressure on the skis.

Her skis fly in the air. Clutching her poles, Maria careens along the icy slope. *Thwack!* She crashes into the red fence. The announcer is stunned. "Oh, what a fall! What a terrible fall! At the same place her teammate Gaffner went down! Just as she was getting to the finish. Maria Walliser really banged into those fences!"

Maria is not badly hurt. But she's bitterly disappointed. She came so close. "I took a risk and went too far." But like a true champion, she looks forward to the next time. "Tomorrow I will not make the same mistake!"

Opposite page: Still clutching her poles as she falls, Maria Walliser plows through the snow as her ski flies into the air. She pushed the limit just a little too far.

ATHLETES HAVE BIG HEARTS — EVEN THE GROUCHY ONES

When people say that Maria Walliser has a big heart, they aren't just talking about how nice she is. They're talking about that powerful muscle pumping blood through her body.

People born with extra-large hearts often make excellent athletes. When he was at his peak, Olympic runner Paavo Nurmi, who won nine gold medals, had a heart that was three times larger than normal. But no matter how large an athlete's heart is, training will strengthen the heart muscle so that it can work harder and more efficiently.

The heart is the main pumping station in the complex network of the circulatory system, which moves blood to and from the lungs and to every single part of the body. This blood system is the highway that brings fuel and oxygen to all our living cells.

The heart has four chambers. Each has a special job. Blood carrying oxygen from the lungs enters the top left chamber. This chamber contracts, squeezing the blood into the lower left chamber. A fraction of a second later, this chamber contracts, pumping the blood into the main artery, the *aorta*. At the same time, the upper chamber relaxes to receive more blood from the lungs.

The aorta leads out of the lower left chamber, in the direction of the head. It branches into several large arteries, the main pipelines that carry blood around the body. Some go directly to the head, others to the upper limbs. One major artery goes down to the lower body. This one divides around the belly button into two branches, one for each leg.

Each artery branches into many smaller arteries, and then into arterioles carrying blood into every area of the body. Arterioles themselves divide into huge numbers of tiny capillaries that deliver blood directly to cells. Although capillaries are the smallest blood vessels in our bodies, they are not the least important. There are so many of them that no part of your body — with a few exceptions like your teeth — is farther from a capillary than the thickness of a page of this book!

Blood in the capillaries delivers oxygen and fuel to cells and picks up waste products, including carbon dioxide. Then it starts the long trip back to the heart through a system of tubes called veins. Blood makes the entire trip from the heart to different parts of the body and back to the heart again in about twenty seconds.

Blood returning from various parts of the body enters the upper right chamber of the heart. The upper right chamber contracts (at the same time that the upper left chamber does), sending the returning blood into the lower right chamber. A fraction of a second later, the lower right chamber contracts (at the same instant that the lower left chamber contracts) and squeezes the returning blood into the lungs. The blood enters the capillaries that pass next to the alveoli. Carbon dioxide leaves the blood, passing through the walls of the capillaries and the alveoli into the lungs, just as new oxygen passes in the opposite direction from the lungs into the blood. The carbon dioxide is pushed out of the body through the nose and mouth when we exhale. Oxygen is brought in with the air when we inhale.

Next time you run to catch a bus or a Frisbee, notice how your body reacts. If you're not in very good physical shape, your heart will pump faster and your lungs will breathe faster. Your pulse will speed up like crazy and you'll be huffing and puffing in no time. But trained athletes have much more control. They have strong heart muscles that can pump more blood with each contraction. So their hearts can beat more slowly. Their lungs can also move more air in and out per minute, because their breathing muscles are stronger. That's why people in good condition don't pant as fast when they exercise as someone who's not fit.

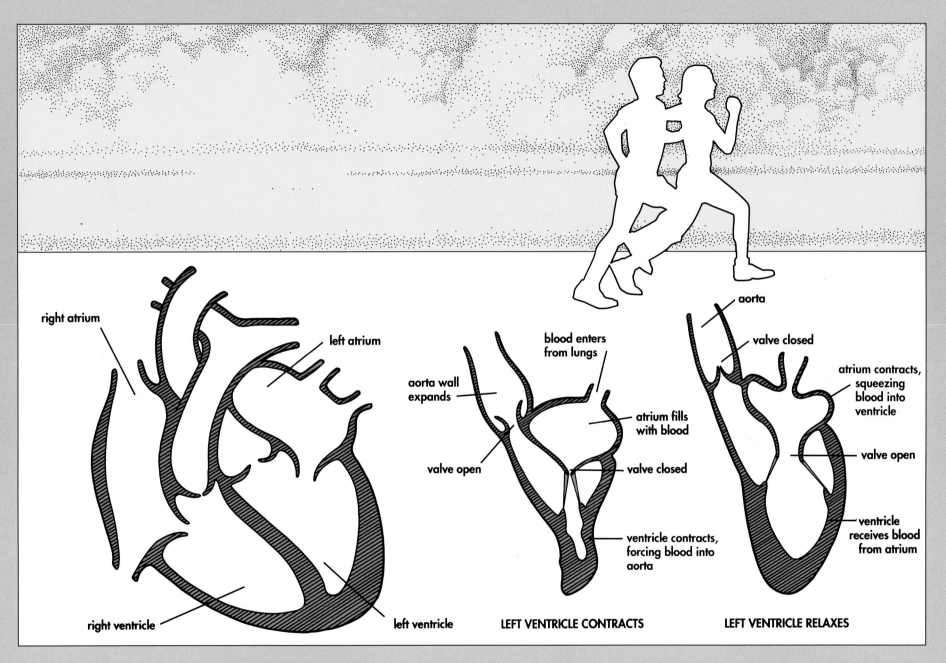

right atrium

left atrium

right ventricle

left ventricle

blood enters
from lungs

aorta wall
expands

valve open

valve closed

atrium fills
with blood

ventricle contracts,
forcing blood into
aorta

LEFT VENTRICLE CONTRACTS

aorta

valve closed

atrium contracts,
squeezing
blood into
ventricle

valve open

ventricle
receives blood
from atrium

LEFT VENTRICLE RELAXES

Above left: *The four chambers of the heart (front view). Blood enters the right atrium from the body. It is pumped down into the right ventricle. Then it is pumped into the lungs, where carbon dioxide is removed and new oxygen is collected. Oxygen-rich blood comes from the lungs into the left atrium. From there it is pumped into the left ventricle, and then out through the aorta to the body.*
Above right: *Pumping action of left atrium and ventricle.*

PERFECTION IN MOTION

Nina Ananiashvili drags herself to the dressing room at the back of the practice hall. She is tired but content. Today's practice was hard, but it went well. She sits down and swings her long legs onto the bench. Stretching like a cat, she leans her flexible body forward, then grabs her toes. They crackle as she bends them back and forth, loosening the muscles and tendons and increasing the flow of blood.

Nina is a prima ballerina with the Bolshoi ballet in Moscow. Tomorrow night she will dance Myrtha in *Giselle*, the oldest ballet in their repertoire. "The part is very difficult, very physical. I will be compared to a hundred years' of Russia's greatest ballerinas."

For a young Russian girl, dancing with the Bolshoi can be the dream of a lifetime. That's how it was for Nina. "I started practicing when I was six, hoping to be chosen." Four years later, she made it. "The Bolshoi has been my home since I was ten."

Years of training are necessary before young dancers go on stage. Their bodies must learn how to move in perfect harmony, not only with themselves but also with the music. "You never dance alone," says Nina. "Always, you are one part of something larger. The orchestra, the dancers around you, the audience. With them all, you belong to a grander, more graceful, more beautiful creature — the ballet." In competitive sports, you know you're the best when you win. In ballet, you can only keep striving for the one goal that can never quite be reached — perfection.

Ballet requires tremendous effort and dedication. Most professional ballet schools accept students at the age of ten. "The young ones practice five hours a day, six days a week," Nina remembers. "They must learn precisely the alphabet of gestures from which they will make words of movement and finally whole poems of ballet."

The basic gestures for ballet are practiced day in and day out for years. First position, second position . . . *demi-plié, grand plié, relevé.* All these terms describe very specific movements the body must learn. Sometimes a student will feel pain even though she is doing the movement correctly. A certain muscle or group of muscles may simply not be accustomed to moving that way. Muscles trained for a new move-

Above: *Prima ballerina Anna Pavlova (1881–1931) in the title role from the famous ballet* The Dying Swan. *She was considered the greatest ballerina of her time.*

Left: *Two young students practicing on the bar at the Bolshoi ballet school in Moscow.*

Opposite page: *Nina Ananiashvili and Erek Mukahamedov practice a difficult movement while their coach looks on. Nina says that "Erek is so strong, so smooth, he makes me feel weightless."*

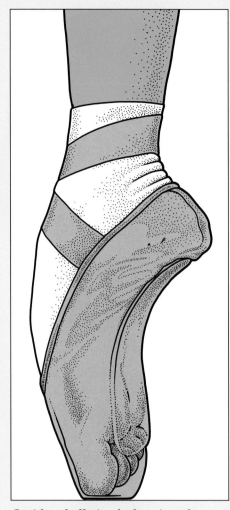

Inside a ballerina's dancing shoes her toes support her entire weight. The best foot for ballet has toes that are about the same length, so the weight is distributed evenly among the toes.

DANCING ON POINTE

To a young girl who wants to be a star in the ballet, the moment of truth comes when her teacher tells her that she's ready to dance on pointe. Finally, she's arrived.

We've all marveled at the ability of ballerinas to dance on their toes. How do they do it? Their secret is practice.

After years of learning to dance in her soft shoes, a young dancer has to learn it all over again on pointe. She works on *pliés* and *relevés*. These are the movements a ballerina makes when she bends her knees then rises up onto her toes. She must also practice the *grands battements*, kicking one leg out straight while staying up on her support leg. Of course, there is also the *pirouette* — a spin while balanced gracefully on the toes of one foot. Finally, when her brain, sensors, and muscles are all working in harmony, she puts the pieces together.

Pointe shoes have no padding in the toes. The part that you stand on, called the block, is like a hard and unyielding cup. Some dancers stuff padding into the toes, but even then they must live with the pain.

Despite the discomfort, young girls dream of dancing on pointe. To them it is like flying. But they quickly learn how difficult it is. Their toes get blisters. Their feet hurt.

If you think dancers' feet have problems, you should see their shoes! When dancers are training hard, they go through pointe shoes really fast. Some have to change pairs two to three times during a performance. A ballet company spends thousands of dollars a year just on shoes.

ment will eventually begin to accept it. The discomfort disappears. In this way, ballet changes the young dancer's body.

Putting the basics together to perform graceful movements is the next step. The body must learn to go from one gesture to another in a smooth, seemingly effortless sequence of moves. The only way is to repeat them over and over again. The endless repetition can be punishing. "Ballet can be very painful," says Nina. "It is not easy to make the difficult look effortless."

The body and the mind have to work together to perform perfect ballet. Every muscle and joint in Nina's body has numerous sensors called *proprioceptors*. They give Nina a sixth sense, a knowledge of where her body is and how it is moving. When Nina learns a new sequence of moves, she first practices each part of it carefully. Her brain stores memories of how each position feels and how her body has to move to the next one. When she is practicing the sequence, her proprioceptors send signals to her brain, telling it how the moves are being performed. The brain compares the signals with memories and images of where Nina wants her body to be. Brain and body send signals back and forth until the movements become almost automatic.

Nina remembers with affection how hard her dance partner, Erek Mukahamedov, worked to perfect his wonderful floating leap. It took him eight long years. Her heart soars when she thinks of how beautiful

Opposite page: *After a long, hard day of practice, Nina's feet can use a good massage.*

SPINNING WITHOUT FALLING

Whirling like a dervish, the dancer spins on the tips of her toes. Around and around she goes, faster and faster. Suddenly, with a flourish, she stops. The music skips lightly along, and she continues her dance.

How do dancers keep their balance? Every one of us has had the experience of spinning around and around. The world turns in front of our eyes, and we get dizzy. If we keep it up for as long as that dancer did, we'd soon crash to the ground.

A dancer uses a special technique to maintain balance during rapid spins. She picks a spot to focus on. As she starts to spin, her head stays still until it can't hold the position any longer. Then she whips her head around and looks at the spot again. This motion, called *spotting*, keeps the visual field steady.

Your body has a similar way of helping you keep your balance when you turn your head. The only difference is that your eyes, not your entire head, make the jerking movement. You can see this reflex in a friend's eyes. Ask him or her to slowly turn around and stare straight ahead the whole time. As his or her eyes go past, you will see them jerking back and forth. The brain knows the head is turning and is telling the eyes to hold still for a moment, then jerk forward, hold still, jerk forward, and so on. This jerking movement helps keep the visual field steady so your friend can keep from falling.

How does your brain know you're turning? You might think your eyes tell it the world is spinning, but that's not how your brain senses the motion. You can prove this for yourself. Close your eyes and hold two fingers lightly on your eyelids. Now slowly turn around with the help of a friend. With your fingertips, you will feel your eyes jerking. The sensors that detect your turning are deep inside your inner ears. They're called the *semicircular canals* and are part of the *vestibular system*.

Dancers often use their eyes to "grab" the world to help keep their balance. When doing spins, they stare at one spot in the distance and snap their heads around on each turn to keep staring at the same spot. This technique is called spotting.

Opposite page: Waiting in the wings on performance night, Nina makes some last-minute adjustments to her shoes. Every last detail must be perfect.

he looks suspended in midair. Not all dancers can perform this amazing feat. As Erek leaps into the air, his mind knows exactly where each part of his body is in space. As he floats upward and gravity begins to pull him down, Erek arches himself and lifts his legs. His body is falling, but his limbs are moving up. It looks as if he is not moving at all. For a brief and wonderful moment, Erek has defied gravity.

Ballet techniques are difficult. It takes years to perfect them, and even the great dancers have to con-

tinue practicing every day. But there's more to ballet than technique. "I practice and practice to achieve perfection," says Nina, "but perfection by itself is a dead thing. I must dance to express emotion." She can hear the voice of her coach talking to her about the roles she will play. It's as if they are real people whom Nina has to become. "She tells me the great ballerinas do not perform — they live."

Pulling herself out of her daydreams, Nina prepares to go home to bed. She must be ready for

Opposite page: *Unaware of the bright stage lights, Nina glides effortlessly through her movements. She has become part of the music, dancing between the notes.*

Below: *Once the curtain is up, Nina is no more. She is now Myrtha, expressing joy and sorrow through the perfection of the dance.*

tomorrow's performance. "Myrtha is the queen of girls with broken hearts. She is very strong, very angry with lost love. I must radiate her power. Tomorrow night, I must become Myrtha." As she drifts off to sleep, Nina enters the imaginary world of the ballet she will perform. She becomes Myrtha as, in her mind, she moves effortlessly through the dance.

The next night, Nina is in costume, waiting backstage. The performance will begin in a few moments. She hears the orchestra tuning up and people in the audience chattering excitedly. Impatiently she paces up and down. Her arms extend outward as she practices a particular move. Her mind focuses on her character. Suddenly the music swells. And Nina is no more. On cue, Myrtha moves past the curtain into the colored lights.

The crowd gasps with pleasure as a figure in white floats onto the stage. Prima ballerina Nina Ananiashvili leaps gracefully into the air. Her body seems to ride on an invisible wave that carries her forward. Her feet hardly touch the ground as she glides effortlessly through a fluid sequence of moves. "When the time comes, I forget what I have learned. I dance between the notes." The audience is rapt with attention. This is ballet at its best. Perfection in motion.

KEEPING YOUR BALANCE

Unless you are lying down, you are continually doing a balancing act. Sitting up, riding a bicycle, or dancing on pointe — all require balance. Gravity is constantly pulling on us. Balance is what keeps us from falling down.

Stand on one leg. Do you notice yourself shifting back and forth? Your brain is comparing the signals coming from different areas of your body and directing your muscles to make any adjustments needed to keep you upright.

A ballerina gracefully poised on the toes of one foot can hold that position for a long time. If you look closely, however, you'll notice tiny adjustments continuously being made. These are the only hint of the vast number of signals running back and forth between the dancer's brain, numerous kinds of sensors, and her well-trained muscles.

Our bodies have three different sensory systems that help us keep our balance. The first system tells us where our body is positioned in space and how it is moving. Every muscle, tendon, and joint has *proprioceptors*, which can detect changes in position and motion. Proprioceptors send electrical signals along nerve cells to a special area in the brain called the *cerebellum*, which coordinates movements. The brain uses this information to tell the muscles what to do.

If you asked a group of people to stand on one leg, you'd notice that some could stay upright longer than others. The better the communication links between a person's proprioceptors and brain, the better a person's balance. You could say they are "well wired." People who have well-developed systems of proprioceptors linked to their brain

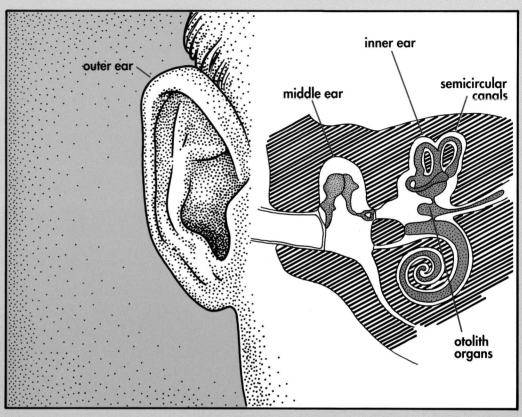

Everyone knows the ears are important for hearing, but few people realize their importance for balance. Complicated sensors in the inner ear detect motions of the head and tell the brain how the head is moving. The semicircular canals detect spin, and the otolith organs detect motion in a straight line.

are naturally athletic. However, training can vastly improve your body awareness. Dancers develop this ability to a very high degree.

The second important system for balance is vision. You can prove this easily. With your eyes open, stand on one leg for as long as you can. Now do it again with your eyes closed. No matter how good you are with your eyes open, you'll have much more trouble without your vision to help you. Dancers doing spins use their vision to help them keep their balance. They focus on one

Perfect balance! This gymnast is using many different parts of his body to keep his balance. Proprioceptors in his muscles, tendons, and joints tell his brain where his limbs are and how they're moving. His eyes watch how the outside world is moving. And sensors in his inner ears measure how his head is moving.

spot, as if they were grabbing it for support.

The third system for balance, called the *vestibular system,* is quite amazing. Smaller than the tip of your finger, two identical sets of sensors are buried deep inside each of your ears. Each set is made of five tiny organs of balance that work together to sense motion of your head. Three of them, the *semicircular canals,* detect rotation (turning and bending). The other two, *otolith organs,* detect straight-line motion. Otolith organs also act as very accurate gravity detectors, so we always know which way is up and which way is down. If you ever lose your balance and start to fall, the vestibular system will tell your brain how your head is moving so it can tell your muscles how to stop your fall.

These three systems of sensors work together to help us keep our balance every day. In some special situations, however, they can fight each other and make a person sick. In the cabin of a ship that's tossing on the open sea, your inner ears sense the rolling motion of your head. They signal your brain to prepare the muscles for a possible fall. Your proprioceptors sense the swaying, too, and they alert the brain as well. But the room looks perfectly normal and your eyes tell your brain that nothing is moving. With these conflicting signals, your brain figures something is wrong.

In some people, the brain responds most to their eyes and acts as if they've drunk alcohol or some other poison that affects their inner ear. The brain tells the stomach to vomit to get rid of the poison, and the person gets sick. Other people have well-developed proprioceptors, and the brain responds to them enough to ignore the eyes. These people are less likely to get seasick. People who do get seasick often go quickly on deck and stare at the horizon, which seems to move up and down as the ship rolls. Now the eyes agree with the other senses. No more disagreements, no more seasickness.

REPROGRAMMING THE BRAIN

Have you ever watched a baby learning to walk? Time after time the baby falls, or goes in the wrong direction. But soon the little tot is walking without even thinking about it — just as you do.

First-rate dancers make their movements appear as effortless as walking. Yet each step is actually impossible to do without months, even years, of training.

When you see a dancer perform, all this work is invisible. Yet in every move and gesture there is practice, practice, and more practice. This is the key to dance.

Each step is broken down into smaller parts. The dancer will study each part until it is perfect, working on each one separately. Proprioceptors in the muscles, tendons, and joints are learning what each correct move feels like. They send this information to the brain, which stores it for later use. Teachers make sure that the dancer does each move

correctly, so that no wrong information is learned.

The next step is to put the pieces together. You can usually pick out dancers who have not quite mastered an entire series of movements. They seem to be thinking their way through the moves. There is a jerky quality to their dancing. Experienced dancers appear more fluid. You can't see the separate steps. The smoothness of the dance comes from the way the body combines the individual parts.

The key is repetition. Once the proprioceptors and brain have learned the steps perfectly, they begin to assemble them into larger units. First the dancer tries a few steps together in a sequence. Over and over

Left: *The brain works with sensors and muscles to make tiny adjustments so the dancer can stand on her toes for a long time.*

Opposite page: *Dancers must train their bodies to hold positions and perform movements that seem awkward at first.*

again, she goes through the series. Her brain combines the familiar pieces into a new pattern of sensations. Eventually the sequence is stored as one new, more complicated step. The dancer gradually builds up bigger and bigger series of steps. Soon the dancer is flowing from one to the next without realizing it.

Teachers tell their dancers to think of the entire dance as a whole, not as a series of steps. Their training helps reprogram dancers' brains to store the dance as if it were one long step. Dancers can tell when they've done it right. It feels terrific!

All artists and athletes use similar training to develop their skills. They break down their moves into small pieces.

An archer practices the draw, the aim, the release. A pianist learns scales, arpeggios, bars, and phrases. A wrestler works on various throws and holds. A skier masters turning and jumping. They learn each piece and how to put them together, then spend the rest of their career trying to forget the little pieces again!

Athletes and other performers who have trained for years begin to feel that all the thinking goes on in their bodies — not their minds. It's what happens when a guitar player says, "My fingers did it," or a runner's legs run the last mile on their own. At the peak of a performance, the mind becomes quiet. One command from the brain — *Do it!* — is enough. And the rest just happens.

STRETCHING YOUR LIMITS

If you could be a champion in any activity, which would you choose? Would it be rock climbing, skiing, dance, or something else? Imagine what your body would be like if you could have that choice. Would it be muscle-bound like a weight lifter's or lean and trim like a runner's?

Some people are born athletes. Canadian Olympic swimmer Alex Baumann won two gold medals in 1984. He's about six feet tall and has huge lungs. They can draw in almost 50 percent more air in one breath than a normal person's can. A person with a large heart will also be a natural athlete, since he or she can pump more blood to bring more oxygen to muscles quickly. Some people are born with a keen body sense. Their sensors communicate well with their brains, and they have naturally good balance.

No matter what body you are born with, training and practice will push you a lot further than natural ability. The maximum capacity of an athlete's lungs will never change, but training will strengthen the diaphragm muscle and the muscles between the ribs so that each breath will be as close to maximum as possible. And trained athletes also have great control, so they can set their breathing rate as fast or as slow as they want, depending on how much oxygen they need and for how long.

Athletes' hearts become stronger. The muscle walls of the heart become thicker, the heart's chambers become larger, and each contraction moves more blood than an untrained heart can. A stronger heart can pump more blood per beat than a normal heart. It can also keep pumping hard for longer periods of time if necessary.

Whatever physical activity you enjoy now or in the future, you can be sure of one thing. If you continue to do it regularly, your body will change. Depending on which sport you do, different muscles will become stronger, and your body may begin to look different.

Rock climber Tony Yaniro has muscular forearms and hands. That's because for more than fifteen years he's been using these parts of his body when he climbs. The muscles of his hands and arms have grown extra capillaries so oxygen-carrying blood can reach the enlarged muscles. Some climbers do chin-ups and other exercises at home to strengthen their muscles. But most find that climbing itself is the best way to keep their climbing muscles in good shape. They find that if they do too many muscle-building exercises, their body weight increases too much for the climb. So you won't find very many climbers with huge upper arms and chests, like wrestlers have.

Maria Walliser gives her legs a tough workout when she skis. Her leg muscles have become large and

Above: In the early 1900s, Saxon Brown — at 17 the "strongest boy in England" — pulls a car weighing over a ton with his teeth.

Opposite page: Cycling is a fine way to condition your body, especially your heart and lungs. Many athletes include cycling as part of their overall training.

powerful. She trains all year round, running to keep her legs in shape and make her lungs and heart work hard. "Strength," she says, "wins races."

A dancer like Nina Ananiashvili has a lean, flexible body. Her sense of balance is highly developed. Years of training for the ballet have changed the way she walks. Her legs and feet are turned out, so that she walks a little like a duck. When she dances, her body can form positions that no one without her training could ever accomplish.

How our bodies develop depends on how we use them. Different activities will cause different muscles to grow and become stronger. But any activity will help your whole body perform better. Almost anything that gives you a good workout will strengthen your heart and your lungs and, therefore, make them work better.

By exercising your lungs and your heart, you increase their ability to help your muscles. A trained athlete's lungs can move more than twice as much

CHANGING YOUR BODY WITH EXERCISE

How is your body different from a pair of shoes? Shoes wear out with use, but the more you use your body, the better shape it will be in.

The best way to build up your muscles is to give them lots of work to do. Weight training actually changes your muscle cells. All muscle cells are long and thin, so they're called fibers. These fibers become thicker with heavy exercise so that when they contract they can supply more power.

If you simply want to do some basic exercises at home, good old-fashioned push-ups, chin-ups, and sit-ups will never let you down. Even if you start with one push-up a day, you'll be surprised how quickly you'll be doing ten, then twenty, then fifty.

Some rock climbers practice a difficult variation on the chin-up. They take a strong board and drill three holes in it for each hand. Then they do chin-ups holding on with only three fingers of each hand. Ouch! This exercise develops strong hands for grabbing small knobs and cracks in the rock.

Running is a terrific way to build up your heart and lungs. If you're a beginner, start slowly by walking longer and longer distances. Then jog gently for about a city block, walk three, and repeat for increasing distances. Finally jog longer distances. Cycling and swimming are also excellent heart and lung exercises, and they aren't as hard on the body as jogging.

Sports and athletic activities like climbing or dancing are fun as well as good for you. If you continue to be active, you'll be amazed at how your body will change over time. But remember: don't overdo it — start with a small number of exercises, and build up your strength slowly but surely.

Above: *Maria Walliser closes her eyes as she mentally practices her run, moving her body back and forth as she makes the turns in her mind.*

Opposite page: *Starting young helps your body learn how to move in different situations. You may be better at one activity than another, but if you work at it, you will be amazed at how your body will respond.*

WATER, WATER

Cooling his jets! This runner soaks his head with water to protect himself against overheating.

No matter how solid you might feel, over 90 percent of your body is made of water. When you exercise, your body uses some of this water as a natural cooling system.

Some of the sweat glands underneath your skin send fluid to the surface through your pores. The liquid appears as perspiration on your skin. As the liquid evaporates, it cools and takes heat from your body.

If you exercise hard for a long period of time, your body can lose a lot of water through perspiration. During a marathon, for example, runners will produce several quarts (liters) of sweat. If too much water is lost, a person becomes dehydrated and his or her health can become endangered.

During very hot weather, the danger of dehydration is greater. If the day is also very humid there is the added danger of heatstroke.

Heatstroke occurs when your working muscles produce too much heat for your body to take away. The perspiration on your skin evaporates very slowly because the air can't absorb any more water. Your body temperature rises, you feel disoriented, you become irritable, and you develop a glassy stare.

For all these reasons athletes make sure that they get enough fluids. If a game or competition lasts a long time, participants try to drink fluids during the event. You can see players taking drinks during a long baseball or football game. Marathon runners often wear headbands, which they soak with water. At feeding stations they also drench their T-shirts, as well as take a good long drink.

air per minute as those of an untrained person. The athlete's heart is stronger and pumps more blood in less time. There are more capillaries around the athlete's muscles, so that plenty of oxygen can get to them fast. Your body will develop the same way if you exercise regularly.

Whatever you do, you don't have to be an all-star athlete or Olympic champion to enjoy using your body. Most people play sports for the fun of it. And even if you can't get the ball in the basket every time, your body will still thank you for pushing it as far as it can go. It may kick and scream a little at first, but the aches and pains will go away, and soon you'll feel much better.

Exercise might even save your life. In the United States, over three-quarters of a million people die each year from diseases of the heart and blood circulation system. Activities that work your heart and muscles regularly, like running, will strengthen your heart and will also change the chemical balance of your body to help protect your blood vessels.

For example, the chemical cholesterol is an important part of all cells and helps carry fatty acids, a source of food energy for cells, in the blood. But too much cholesterol in the blood can cause problems. If it collects in the walls of a blood vessel, the walls will gradually become thicker and will block the easy flow of blood. If the blood vessels that bring oxygen to the heart muscle become very narrow, blood and oxygen have difficulty getting to the heart,

Opposite page: *Active bodies respond well to being pushed and will be healthier.*

and a person develops a risk of having a heart attack. Scientists have shown that long-distance running can change the chemistry of the blood so that cholesterol is less likely to collect in the walls of blood vessels.

Even though exercise will make you healthier, overdoing it can cause you harm. One danger is overheating. If you exercise too long and hard on a hot day, the heat produced by your working muscles might not be able to escape fast enough. If your body temperature goes up too high, you might trigger a systems breakdown. All of the ways your body gets rid of heat (like perspiration) start to fail, and you can suffer heatstroke. Marathon runners make sure that they drink fluids before and during the race to avoid dehydration and to keep their bodies cool. They also splash water on their bodies so that evaporation can carry away some of the heat. In general, if you're careful and take the proper precautions, sports and exercise will make your body much healthier.

The good effects of proper exercise are often more noticeable when you stop exercising after having done it for a while. If you get sick or have an injury that puts you in bed for some time, you'll notice that your body has gotten out of shape. When athletes suffer a leg or back injury, their trainers usually try to get them moving as soon as possible. Otherwise it may take them months after the injury is healed to get back to normal.

It's especially important for people who can't move around easily to push their bodies as much as possible. Active bodies respond well to being pushed and will be healthier. That's the reason people who have a physical handicap try to stay as active as they can. Imagine losing an arm or a leg in an accident. Until quite recently, you would have had to sit at home with little chance to exercise. Today there are many runners and skiers with one leg, and special competitions are often held for physically challenged people who want to push their limits. Some sports clubs organize basketball games and other activities for people confined to wheelchairs.

Opposite page: A skier with one leg speeds down the slalom course.

THE RUNNING "HIGH"

During a long run, natural painkillers called endorphins are released into the brain.

Many runners simply have to run. It's almost as if they were addicted to running, just as a person gets addicted to a drug. Is there possibly some connection to a real drug? The answer is yes. When muscles get tired, a type of nerve called a pain receptor sends signals to the brain that we experience as pain. If we feel too much pain, we stop using the muscle, and it is able to rest.

There are chemicals in the brain called *endorphins*, which can control the information the brain receives from pain receptors. One of the most powerful painkillers used today, called morphine, is similar to endorphins.

During a long run like the marathon, the brain increases the amount of endorphins it makes. This naturally produced drug reduces the effect of the signals coming from the pain receptors in the muscles. Runners can feel the results as a gradual disappearing of the pain that has been building during their run. Many marathoners say a feeling of happiness comes over them as the pain goes away, and they get an extra burst of energy to keep going. That's probably one of the reasons that marathoners can run such long distances.

CHANGING WORLD RECORDS — IS THERE A LIMIT?

The year is 1896. The place is Athens, Greece. The event — the first modern Olympics. Runners are lined up for the 100-meter dash. The gun goes off. The runners take off. American Thomas Burke wins in 12 seconds flat.

Since that first 100-meter win by Burke, no Olympic sprinter has run that slowly. Gold-medalist sprinters are running faster and faster each year. High jumpers are clearing greater heights. What causes these changes?

Sometimes it's a new technique. In the high jump, American Richard Fosbury won a gold medal and international fame in 1968 with his "Fosbury flop." This new technique of rolling over the bar was laughed at by international coaches at first. But by 1980, thirteen of the sixteen Olympic finalists were using it!

Another way to improve performance is training. Modern athletes use sensors and computers to track what their bodies are doing during practice. Their coaches figure out how often and how long they should train, how hard, and what techniques they should use. Over time, performance can be greatly improved.

For all these reasons and more, athletes' performances are improving from year to year. The speeds have been getting faster and faster, the distances greater and greater, the times shorter and shorter. One wonders if the athletes will keep getting better and better, or if we'll find there's a limit to what we can do.

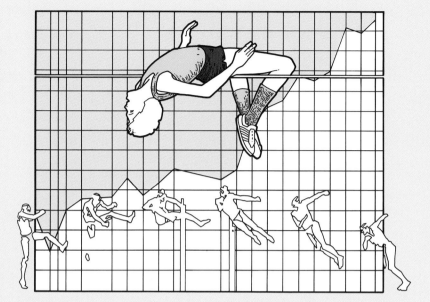

In 1968, American high jumper Richard Fosbury wowed Olympic watchers with a new way of clearing the bar. His "Fosbury flop" won him a gold medal and a world record. His new method is shown at top, the old way of high jumping at bottom.

People with physical handicaps face challenges every day. Some set themselves even greater ones that inspire us all. Terry Fox was an extraordinary athlete. Even though he had cancer, he continued to run. When his doctors had to amputate one of his legs, he decided to do something to encourage and help others. He set out to run right across his native country, Canada, which spans a whole continent. He was able to make it halfway before the cancer came back, and he had to stop. Terry is remembered by people around the world for his courageous accomplishment.

Every one of us has something of Terry Fox inside.

Child or adult, amateur or champion, we search for our limits. From step to stride to leap, we push ourselves to new heights. And just when we think maybe we'll never make it, a whole new world opens up. We discover new strengths, new abilities, new possibilities. Our bodies become stronger, our minds more agile. With each breakthrough we experience a profound joy that makes the struggle to be our best worth the effort. It's what makes us continue to push to the limit.

Opposite page: Reaping the rewards. Tony Yaniro enjoys the spectacular view after a tough climb.

SWIMMING AND CYCLING YOUR WAY TO THE MARATHON

Long-distance runners love the feeling they get when they run. But many of them hurt themselves by running too much.

In the 1980s athletes used to believe that the best way to train for a marathon was to run, run, run your heart out. But more and more people are realizing that the body will do better with a range of activities. For one thing, if you don't exhaust your body from too much running, you will get fewer injuries. And the fewer injuries you get, the more you can train. But more than that, practicing several sports — called cross-training — can make you a better runner.

Frank Shorter won the Olympic marathon in 1972. During training for the event he ran three times a day. After his Olympic win, he ran only twice a day, which was the standard amount. Now he trains by running in the morning and bicycling in the afternoon. No more second run. He claims that he's fitter overall and that his running has improved.

Marathon runners typically do a combination of speed running (sprinting) and long-distance running during their training. The speed work is punishing on the legs, and athletes usually have to wait a week between tough workouts. Frank just hops on his bike, which allows him to vary his workout with less risk of injury.

Some runners use swimming in the same way Frank uses cycling. In the water, your legs don't have to support your weight. Swimming fast is good exercise for your lungs and heart but doesn't give your legs

Right: *Champion skier Maria Walliser runs regularly as part of her training. Here she is jog-jumping, a strenuous combination of jumping and running that strengthens her legs and her heart.*

the pounding that a run will. Some athletes swim laps. Others, like 1984 gold medalist marathoner Joan Benoit Samuelson, "water run." Joan wears a Wet Vest that keeps her body upright when she's in the water. Then she moves her arms and legs in the same way that she would while running on land. The only difference is that her legs don't hit the ground. "A half hour in the pool feels like a 15-mile run for me," says Joan.

Alpine skier Leslie Krichko needed an accident to force her to change her ways. Leslie is a three-time Olympic medal winner. Like most skiers, she used to train by skiing in winter and running in summer. But in 1987 she injured her foot and couldn't run or ski. By using an Aquajogger, invented by exercise physiologist Dick Brown, Leslie was able to train hard enough to qualify for the 1988 Olympic team for her native country, Norway.

The resistance of water is over ten times greater than air, so it's easy to get your heart pumping and your lungs puffing. Athletes run in water smoothly and slowly, working their muscles against the water. Skiers make the same movements they would while cross-country skiing. Some skiers pretend they are running through a bunch of tires laid out on the ground, just as football players do when training for balance, speed, and rhythm. Most athletes who train in water also make sure to do land training, especially cycling.

Running, cycling, and swimming are the most popular cross-training activities because they keep the lungs and heart working. Weight training is also used to keep muscles in good shape. When athletes return to practice their main sport, they feel refreshed and in top physical condition.

Cross-training can help athletes improve their performance by breaking free from their usual routine and by helping them to stay in shape with less risk of injury. But if they're training for a competition, their primary activity should be in their specific sport. The muscles you use when you are rock climbing, for instance, are best developed by climbing rocks. If you go to the gym and do bench presses or chin-ups, it isn't quite the same. Sure, you make some muscles stronger; but not all the same ones in the same combination that you use during a good climb. Hockey players train by skating and playing hockey. Swimmers swim. Runners run. So athletes tend to train and train some more in their own sport.

Of course, there are athletes who don't use cycling or swimming just as a break from running. They train seriously for the triathlon — a grueling Olympic event in which contestants have to run, swim, and cycle long distances. Some people think triathloners are even crazier than marathoners!

Maybe these serious athletes are just learning all over again what every kid knows. Kids don't specialize in one thing. They try out different activities. Sports are fun, and the more you try, the more you can enjoy!

CREDITS

L	Left
R	Right
T	Top
B	Bottom

Photographs from the film *To The Limit*, distributed by *MacGillivray Freeman Films*:

Front and back cover, cover, title page, contents page, and pages **i, 7, 8, 9, 11, 14, 17, 19, 20L, 21, 22 L, 22 R, 23, 28, 31, 32 R, 33, 35, 38, 39 L, 41, 42 R, 43, 44 B, 45, 48, 49 B, 50, 53, 55, 57, 59, 60 R, 61 L, 62, 63**

Photograph from The St. John Group:

Page 10 L

Photograph from Canapress Photo Service/Dave Buston:

Page 26 R

Photographs from Canada Wide Feature Services Limited:

Page 27 R, **30** L, **47** L, **54** L, **56** L

Photographs from The Bettmann Archive, UPI, and Reuters Photo Libraries:

Page 5 L, **5** R, **10** R, **15** L, **29** L, **39** R, **51** R

Right: *A curtain call for Nina Ananiashvili.*

Opposite page: *Erek Mukahamedov of the Bolshoi performs a floating leap.*

INDEX

ABOUT THIS BOOK

This book is based on the award-winning motion picture *To The Limit*, created by the Museum Film Network and NOVA/WGBH Boston. The film was produced by MacGillivray Freeman Films. The film script was written by Jon Boorstin based on an idea by Paula S. Apsell. The publishers wish to acknowledge the filmmakers, including producer and director Greg MacGillivray, executive producers Paula S. Apsell and Jeffrey W. Kirsch, and senior producer Susanne Simpson. Special acknowledgment goes to Donald M. Berwick, M.D., scientific adviser for the film. Special thanks to David Barlow, Ph.D, who is responsible for the endoscopic images that appear in the film and are reprinted here.

To The Limit is a celebration of how the body works and an exploration of the limits of human performance. Endoscopic photography provides remarkable inside-the-body views that illustrate critical moments in the biology of physical performance. The threshold of technology was taken to the limit to film this extraordinary footage and to project the images eight stories tall onto the IMAX® screen. *To The Limit* premiered in March 1989 and has been projected in OMNIMAX theaters in many cultural and entertainment centers around the world.